Designed by Flowerpot Press
www.FlowerpotPress.com
CHC-0909-0593
ISBN: 978-1-4867-2585-4
Made in China/Fabriqué en Chine

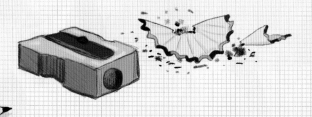

# HOW DO YOU SHARE WITH YOUR FRIENDS?

## A MATH BOOK ABOUT FRACTIONS, DECIMALS, & PERCENTS

written by
lucy d. hayes
illustrated by
srimalie bassani

Fractions as Nu...

Fractio...

1/2        one-

2/         two-

1/         one-

two-

Randomly pick to win a special gift!

Good luck, Suzy!

special surprise

I love math!

How do you share with your friends? Sharing is caring. Well that's what my teachers always say, and so far I've found it to be true! Whenever I have friends over I love to share my toys and snacks with them, and I always want to make sure I do so fairly and evenly.

So how do you share with your friends? Do you get an automatic share sorter?

While that does seem pretty useful, I don't think it's a real thing. When you are sharing, all you are really doing is taking whatever you have and splitting it up evenly with the people you are sharing with. To truly understand how to share, we need to be able to talk about fractions, decimals, and percents. These are the three different ways we talk about pieces of a whole or parts of a group.

We could all practice sharing by eating this delicious cake!

How do you share cake with your friends? Do you just let everyone dig in? Well you can, but you can also use fractions to divide up your whole cake into equal pieces.

Are you ready to bake our cake?

Here we go!

The final touches!

Imagine the end of the year is around the corner and your class is throwing an end-of-school party. You spend all day Sunday baking with your dad, and you make a delicious chocolate cake to share with all your classmates. How do you know how to cut the cake evenly so that all of your classmates can have a slice?

I can't wait to share my cake!

One whole cake!

1

# FRACTIONS

Before you cut your cake, you have one whole cake. One is a whole number. If you wanted to share your cake with just your dad, you would cut your cake straight down the middle and have two equal halves. One half is a fraction of a number. You write fractions like this: $\frac{1}{2}$.

If four of your classmates are sharing your cake, you are going to need to slice it into four even parts. If you take one slice for yourself, you have one out of four ($\frac{1}{4}$) slices of cake. That's also a fraction! A fraction tells you how many pieces you have of a whole.

$\frac{1}{2}$

$\frac{1}{2}$

$\frac{1}{2}$

Me

Dad

Me

Michael

$\frac{1}{4}$

$\frac{1}{4}$

$\frac{1}{4}$

$\frac{1}{4}$

$\frac{1}{4}$

Noah

Mia

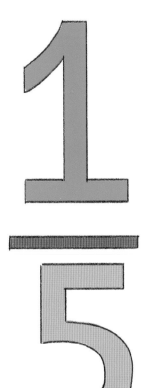

**numerator**

The 1 that you see on the top of this fraction is called a numerator. A numerator represents how many pieces of a whole you have.

**fraction bar**

**denominator**

The 5 that you see on the bottom of this fraction is called a denominator. A denominator represents the total number of pieces that make up the whole.

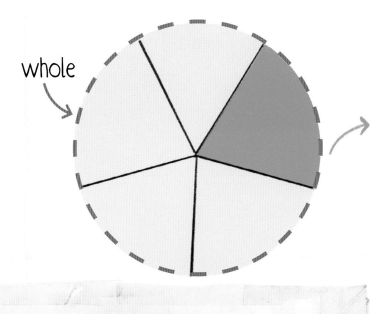

whole

→ **1 out of 5 equal parts**

The fraction $\frac{1}{5}$ means that you have one out of five pieces!

I can finish my half of the pizza tomorrow!

Maybe I can finish your half of the pizza now!

How do you talk about fractions? Is that even allowed? Of course it is! It's easy!

Fractions actually come up a lot when we speak. Have you ever heard someone say, "I am going to save half of my pizza for later" or "I am seven and a half years old"? Those are examples of fractions!

My name is Olivia, and I am seven and a half years old.

You also hear people talk about fractions when they are talking about time. For example, if your parent tells you that you and your brother can have half an hour to read before bed, that's a fraction too.

You can use any combination of numbers to make a fraction, as long as you are talking about pieces of a whole. For example, if you and your dad made a cake with 24 total pieces to share with your class, then each of your classmates would get $\frac{1}{24}$ of the cake.

Here are some examples of fractions you might commonly see:

| Fractions as Numbers | Fractions as Words |
|---|---|
| 1/2 | one-half |
| 2/3 | two-thirds |
| 1/4 | one-fourth |
| 2/5 | two-fifths |

# DECIMALS

How do you share money with your friends? Do you cut a dollar bill into the number of pieces you need? No way! Before you cut your dollar into pieces, try learning about decimals!

Imagine your friends come over to play on a hot summer day and you decide to start a lemonade stand. You sell each cup of lemonade for $1. If you want to share the money you have made evenly between you and your three friends, then you will each get one-fourth of a dollar.

The decimals in money mean that you have part of one hundred. Decimals are written with a decimal point that separates whole numbers from parts of numbers. One dollar has the same value as 100 pennies. If you have one penny, you have 1/100th of a dollar, which you could write as the decimal 0.01, or $0.01 cent.

If you are splitting one dollar between four people, you will each have 25 of the 100 pennies that make up one whole dollar. This means you each have $0.25 cents. If you and your friends make $5.00 total from your lemonade stand, you will each make one whole dollar and 25 cents, or $1.25.

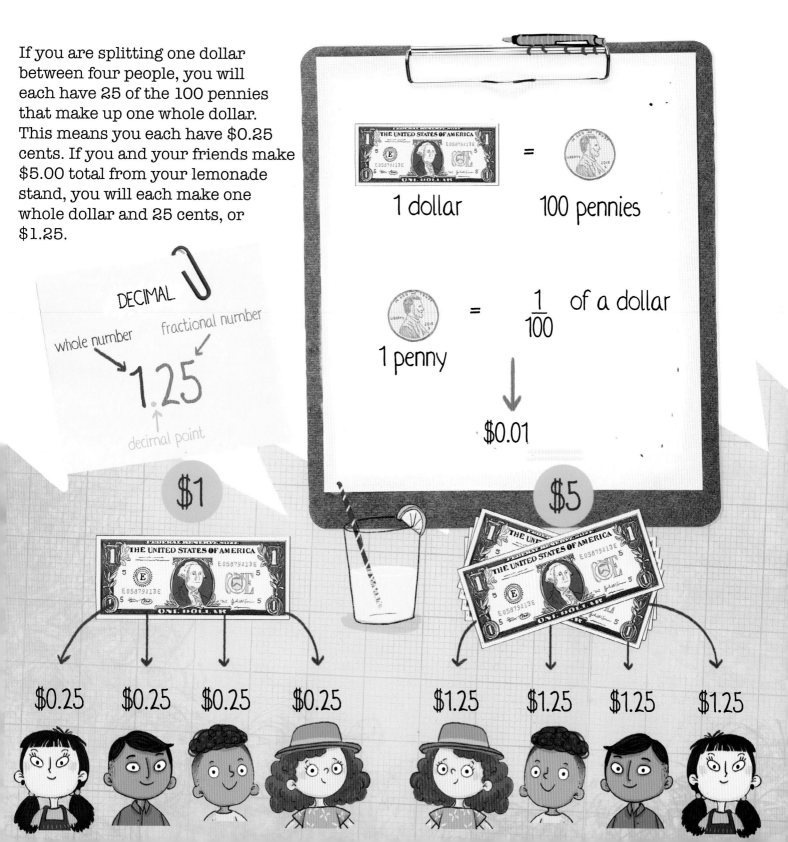

1 dollar = 100 pennies

1 penny = $\frac{1}{100}$ of a dollar

$0.01

DECIMAL

whole number ↘ fractional number ↙

1.25

↑ decimal point

$1

$5

$0.25    $0.25    $0.25    $0.25    $1.25    $1.25    $1.25    $1.25

100 pennies    20 nickels    10 dimes    4 quarters

When it comes to money, decimals represent all of the numbers between 0 and 1. You can use decimals to represent any piece of 100, but money represents lots of the common decimal points! We already know that one dollar is the same as 100 pennies, but one dollar is also the same as four quarters, 10 dimes, or 20 nickels.

If you have one quarter, you have $0.25 cents. If you have two quarters, you have $0.50 cents. If you have three quarters, you have $0.75 cents. And if you have four quarters, you have one whole dollar ($1.00)! One dime means you have $0.10, and one nickel means you have $0.05. Make sense?

Wow, this thing is getting pretty heavy!

# DECIMALS IN MONEY

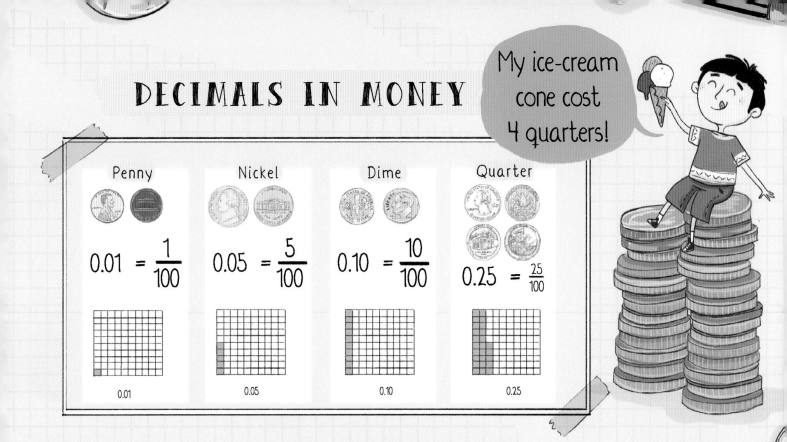

My ice-cream cone cost 4 quarters!

| Penny | Nickel | Dime | Quarter |
|---|---|---|---|
| $0.01 = \dfrac{1}{100}$ | $0.05 = \dfrac{5}{100}$ | $0.10 = \dfrac{10}{100}$ | $0.25 = \dfrac{25}{100}$ |
| 0.01 | 0.05 | 0.10 | 0.25 |

If you have a combination of pennies, nickels, dimes, and quarters, you can still use decimals to talk about how much money you have. In that case, you would just need to do some addition to figure it out.

If you have 1 quarter, 1 dime, 1 nickel, and 1 penny, how much money do you have in total? Add up the decimals to find out.

$0.25 cents + $0.10 cents + $0.05 cents + $0.01 cent = $0.41 cents

# PERCENTS

How do you split up jobs and chores with your friends? Do you play rock, paper, scissors to see who does all the cleaning? You could, or you could all pitch in. Percents can help you split up the work!

Think about your lemonade stand from earlier. After you sell out of lemonade, you and your friends may decide to share the job of cleaning up all the lemons you used. If you split the job up evenly, you can get it done quickly.

Percent really means "per cent" or a number out of 100, just like one cent is one penny out of the 100 pennies that make up a dollar.

LEMONADE

sold out

Fresh Lemonade
$1 for 1 cup

I'm 100% sure we should all help out!

# PERCENTS

percent symbol 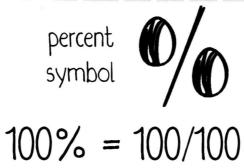 %

$$100\% = 100/100$$

$$40\% = 40/100$$

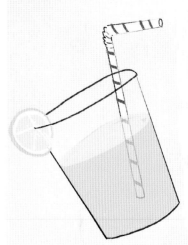

Let's clean this mess up together!

When you are writing a percent, you use a number and the percent sign (%). For example, if you and your friends want to clean up all the lemons you used, you would say you need to clean up 100% of the lemons.

If you are splitting the clean-up job with your three friends, you will each need to clean up 25% of the lemons. This is because 25 is one-fourth of the whole clean-up job.

25 lemons

100 lemons

25 lemons

25 lemons

25 lemons

**50%**

What percent of lemons do you think you have cleaned up if two of your friends have finished their work and two of you have not started? You guessed it! You have cleaned up 50% of the lemons.

**75%**

If three of you have finished cleaning up your portions of the lemons, you have cleaned up 75% of the lemons.

**100%**

Finally, if you have all finished your individual tasks, you have cleaned up 100% of the lemons. Now you can go play!

You may have noticed that fractions, decimals, and percents all seem to go together. That's because they do! They are all parts of a whole.

Think about your cake from earlier. If you cut your cake into four even pieces and you have one slice, then you have $\frac{1}{4}$ of a whole cake. This is the same as having 0.25 of the cake or 25% of the cake.

whole cake

split into 4 equal pieces

$\frac{1}{4}$ of whole cake

25% of whole cake

0.25 of whole cake

Let's look at another example. If your mom asks you to clean your room and the kitchen before going outside to play, then you have two jobs standing between you and outdoor fun. If you complete one of the two jobs then take a break, then you have completed half $(\frac{1}{2})$ of the jobs. This is the same as completing 0.50 of the jobs or 50% of the jobs. Isn't it cool how you can use fractions, decimals, and percents to represent the same situation?

I can do it!

If you only clean one room, you have completed $\frac{1}{2}$ or 0.50 or 50% of the job!

whole sandwich

sandwich split into 4 equal pieces

How do you know when to use a fraction, decimal, or percent? Do you just take a guess? Sort of!

Depending on what you are talking about, there are common times to use one or the other.

Just half an hour left!

# FRACTIONS

Fractions show up when you are trying to share food with your friends or hear an adult talking about time.

For example, if you have a sandwich and you want to share it with your sister and two brothers, you will need to cut it so that you can each have $\frac{1}{4}$. If you are driving home from a road trip and ask your mom how long it will take you to get home, she may say "half an hour." And if you love playing soccer, you might get oranges at halftime.

Time for a break!

These are my favorite ice cream flavors by how much of each I put in my bowl!

- chocolate
- mint chocolate chip
- coconut
- peanut butter

$\frac{1}{4}$

$\frac{1}{2}$

$\frac{1}{8}$

$\frac{1}{8}$

# DECIMALS

Decimals show up when you are talking about money and taking measurements. If you are wanting to buy lunch with your friends, you may see decimals in the prices of the food you are going to buy. For example, a sandwich could cost $1.25. If you are measuring the length of your little brother's hair, you may find it is 2.25 inches (5.72 centimeters) long.

# PERCENTS

Sometimes you'll see percents when you get your grades in school, when you are shopping at the mall, and when you are charging your electronics. If you get 19 out of 20 questions right on a spelling test, then you get 95%!

If you are buying new toys at the mall, you may be able to get more if you find the 40% off sale section.

Is the bear on sale?

Yes, it is 40% off!

teddy bear
$5

100% fun!

I am 100% sure I got a great deal on this super cute teddy bear!

If you want to play video games on a road trip, you will need to charge your device to 100%.

100%

# PIZZA PARTY FRACTIONS

Practice your fractions by making a yummy pizza to share with your friends.
As you read through the recipe, you may notice some fractions and decimals.

**PREP TIME:** 5 minutes

**COOK TIME:** 30 minutes

## INGREDIENTS:

1 round (14.0-ounce to 16.0-ounce) premade pizza crust
(you can also make your own dough at home)

1 $\frac{1}{2}$ cups of marinara sauce

8.0 ounces of shredded mozzarella cheese

Preferred toppings (Try onions, mushrooms, bacon, red peppers, chicken, sausage, pepperoni, pineapple, ham, or anything else you like!)

Ask an adult for help with this activity!

# INSTRUCTIONS

1. Preheat your oven to 475°F. Line a large baking sheet with parchment paper.

2. Place the pizza crust on your baking sheet.

3. Spread marinara sauce evenly over your crust.

4. Sprinkle shredded cheese evenly over your crust.

5. Add preferred toppings! For this step, try dividing your pizza into fractions. Put your first topping on $\frac{1}{2}$ of your pizza. Put your second topping on $\frac{1}{4}$ of your pizza. Put your third and fourth toppings each on $\frac{1}{8}$ of your pizza.

6. Have an adult transfer your baking sheet to the oven. Bake your pizza for 30 minutes or until the crust is golden-brown and the cheese is completely melted.

7. Have an adult remove your pizza from the oven and let it cool for 5 minutes.

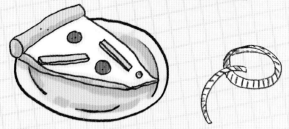

8. Slice your pizza into different fractions based on how many people you are sharing your pizza with!

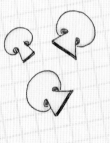

# COLORFUL GRIDS USING PERCENTS

Create a masterpiece using what you know about percents.

## WHAT YOU WILL NEED:

- a piece of grid paper with 100 squares (You can create your own or ask a parent or guardian to help you download one from online.)

- colored pencils, markers, or crayons

46%!

# INSTRUCTIONS

1. Pick a percent. It can be 10%, 20%, 30%, or even 80%.

2. Once you have chosen a percent, figure out how many out of 100 that percent represents. (If you chose 30%, then that would be 30 out of 100.) Now that you have your magic number, choose a color to represent that number.

3. Use your chosen color to color in the same number of squares as your number. You can color any squares you want.

4. Color the remaining squares with another color to see your creation. Your art represents the percent you chose!

5. Try choosing another percent and making a new piece of artwork!

51%!

# FRACTIONS, PERCENTS, & DECIMALS

Here are some common fractions, decimals, and percents and how they relate to one another. Use this chart as a reference.

| FRACTION | PERCENT | DECIMAL |
|:---:|:---:|:---:|
| 1 | 100% | 1.00 |
| 1/2 | 50% | 0.50 |
| 1/3 | 33.3% | 0.333 |
| 1/4 | 25% | 0.25 |
| 1/5 | 20% | 0.20 |
| 1/6 | 16.6% | 0.166 |
| 1/8 | 12.5% | 0.125 |
| 1/10 | 10% | 0.10 |
| 1/12 | 8.3% | 0.083 |